BREATH

The inner essence of

meditation and prayer

Jonas Yunus Atlas

BREATH: THE INNER ESSENCE OF MEDITATION AND PRAYER
Jonas Yunus Atlas

*

Yunus Publishing

*

ISBN(print): 978-90-814-9961-3
ISBN (epub): 978-15-022-8753-3
ASIN (Kindle): B00QZD9IWW
D/2014/12.808/2

*First published in Dutch
as "Geen adem behalve de adem. Mediteren"
Averbode, 2007*

*Previously published in English
as "The little book of prayer and meditation."
Yunus Publishing, 2011*

*

*

*www.jonasatlas.net
www.yunuspublishing.org*

*

Cover image
© kristo74 | Adobe Stock

As Mahatma Gandhi said:
"Prayer is a longing of the soul.
Thus it is better in prayer
to have a heart without words
than words without a heart."

Contents

Preface...1

Guidelines..7

Commencing..33

One point meditation..45

Unity meditation...73

Emptiness meditation...91

Prayer...97

Concluding..117

Preface

This book elucidates the flow of our mind, heart and soul during meditation and prayer. It wishes to explain how we can guide our inner being to moments of spiritual contemplation.

As such, this book does not discuss the outer forms or technical sides of meditation and prayer, but reveals their mental forms and deeper spirit. It explains their underlying spiritual attitude because, in the end, these are spiritual and not physical acts. Many meditation books focus on bodily exercises and physical postures that would be needed to open distinct energy channels. Those certainly can be useful, but they do not necessarily lead to true meditation or prayer since meditation and prayer are above all a matter of different 'spiritual postures' that open the 'channels of the soul' between ourselves and God.

*

The different chapters of this book are not drawn up according to some strict structure. Because of the spiritual composition there are of course some parallels, symmetries and links to be found, but there was no intention of offering any chronological, psychological or theological composition. The imposition of such a structure would lead to nothing but an illusion in any case.

There are no different 'phases', therefore, that are to be traversed one after the other, as if the book builds up to the highest and most sublime goal. All forms of meditation and prayer are of equal value in their proper time and place.

Only the chapters about 'commencing' and 'concluding', which are of course meant to clarify how one should start and close a meditation or prayer session, are put at the beginning and the end of this book for obvious reasons.

The chapters on 'commencing' are also preceded by some chapters on general guidelines. These describe particular fundamental concepts one should take into account when getting involved with meditation and prayer. It will be evident that these are not forms of meditation as such, but simply some important underlying considerations.

In the rest of the book, every new little chapter describes another form of meditation or prayer. They are grouped according to the general 'form' that underlies them, but in principle they all stand by themselves.

You, the reader, are invited to 'test' and 'try' some of the various meditation and prayer types at different times. Perhaps a particular form does not suit you. Then leave it behind after one or a couple of meditation sessions. But perhaps it does fit your spiritual need of the moment. Then you might wish to enjoy and 'use' it for a longer time. Or maybe you find yourself struggling with a certain form but do feel it has much value. Then once in a while spend some more time on it to really understand and taste its fruit.

*

A last preliminary remark is this: this book should be taken in slowly. It should be chewed upon and digested well. Meditation and prayer should lead to inner peace, and inner peace, as everybody knows, does not spring from haste.

Guidelines

As Jalal ad-Din Rumi said:
"When somebody sprinkles musk-scent over the blind man,
the blind man thinks it originates out of himself and not
out of the friendliness of his friend."

Openness

To meditate is to be open.
Be open,
and receptive.

Those who do not open their hearts,
are not able to meditate.

Those who do not open to God,
will never be able to experience His Love.

Those who aren't open,
only seek themselves.

How absurd it is to seek yourself
— you are yourself already.
Why would you need to look for yourself?
How can you look past yourself?
You are confronted with yourself
every second of the day.

Meditation is the search
for the ground of your being,
for the source of what drives you.
It is the search for the cause of struggle
and the possibility of peace.

And all of this does not only reside within the self
but also without.

Those who aren't open to what comes from outside,
suffocate and rust.

The water will make you rust when you're closed
but it will quench your thirst
if you're prepared to drink.

Therefore,
be receptive.

God

Faith in God
is not a prerequisite
for meditation.

God is but a name
for the deepest depth of existence
for the mystical mystery
for the eventual love
that's both the source and the connection
of creation.

God is but a name
for the wave
that brings people closer
that drives the essence of our being forward
that forms the undercurrent
of all that surrounds us with beauty.

Meditation and prayer
are difficult for those who sense nothing
of that deepest depth,
that mystical mystery,
that eventual love,
that wave,
that drive,
or that undercurrent.
Yet, an experience of even the tiniest part suffices
to understand.

Everyone perceives God but partly.
The part we realise
does not have to conform
to the vision of others.

Yet the different parts connect
here and there
now and then.
It allows all of us
to point towards the same reality.

For within reality
something is more present than any presence.
And that presence within reality
is what religions call God.

Techniques and teachers

Techniques do not bring you closer to God.
The art of giving and living does.

It's like being in love.
A technique will never bring you to God
unless applied by a fertile mind.

A dry and frozen mind
that aims for God with planned intention
will never taste His unexpected sweetness
just like a dry and frozen lover
will never feel the rapture of passion.

What matters is not what you do,
but the amount of love you do it with.

The techniques of meditation
thus are the slaves of its spirit.

Integrate the techniques in your contemplation
but keep your mind focussed on God
not on your actions.

Find yourself a teacher
to teach you techniques
but do not become dependent
on him or his methods.

Find yourself a teacher
because God reveals Himself through teachers
but never limit God
to the words or person that revealed Him.

Neither you nor your teacher are the true instructor.
In the end there is only one true teacher
and that is God Himself.

God gives and teaches
the one that seeks for truth
just like the mother gives milk
to the child that wishes to grow.

Religion

Meditation and prayer
cannot be removed
from their religious roots and surrounding.

The one who cuts the flower from the stem
will soon see it wither.

Meditation is not self-help therapy.
It's an inner wrestling
with yourself, your neighbour and God.

That wrestling has been wrestled for centuries.
Many have done it before you.

That is why meditation is embedded
in tradition and wisdom.
It's embedded in acts and deeds of many souls
that lived and loved throughout the centuries.

Every form of meditation and prayer
has its origin and aim.
The one who separates them of these
separates them of their fundaments and roof.
Though your house will be built quickly,
from all sides rain will enter
and your house will slowly collapse.

Build in God and his expressions through religion
your house will stand strong and protected.

Nonetheless,
the believe in God is not the issue.
How you exactly call it or leave it wordless,
how you exactly describe it or leave it imageless
does not matter.

What matters is *that* you adhere to religion,
not to *which*.

Not the names or description
but the depth of what moves you within
will determine your progress.

As the Buddha said:

"Your thoughts are like fish stranded on the shore, that wriggle and quiver. Enemies that hate each other can maim, hurt and kill, but far bigger is the destruction in one's own soul of an unpeaceful mind."

Thoughts

Never force your mind
to become empty
but also never let your mind
go its own way unrestrained.

It's of no use to get angry
with yourself
when you cannot seem to get rid
of all those thoughts.
Yet it's also useless to put no limits
to yourself
when you cannot seem to get rid
of all those emotions.

Attacking your thoughts aggressively
only brings new frustrations
and even more thoughts.
To live out all your desires
only brings new expectations
and even more desires.

Call your thoughts and feelings to order.
Be firm and honest with yourself.
That takes practice, perseverance and friendliness.
Be friendly with yourself.
You do not have to hit yourself or your mind.
You do not have to push it like a donkey.

The mind is often confused and chaotic.
That is how it is.
Forgive your own mind,
accept the fact that you are normal
and begin again.

Peace and calmness originate
when one is friendly enough
to always try again.

Only patience
conquers a restless mind
just like only love
transforms hate,
just like only the unity of God
heals division
— from the inside yet embracing,
slowly yet resolute.

Energy

Energy flows through your body
with just as much certainty
as the fact that you breathe air.
The one who denies the existence of Qi or Praña
is just as blind as the man who closes his eyes
and says the sun doesn't shine.

Through concentration and contemplation
you naturally arouse more energy.
As long as both your mind and body are open,
you will feel its flow.

It will flow through you
and entwine your body and mind.
It will flow in and out
and bring you greater unity.

But whatever you feel,
never lose yourself in the feeling.
Always be conscious
that the experience you have
is not your goal.
Receive it in all its beauty.
Receive it with joy.
But never seize it as yours
and always let it go
when, once again,
it flows away.

Do not cramp your attention
on energetic or astral tricks.
Otherwise you'll be nothing
but a circus dog of your ego.

Striving for power is just as ruinous in meditation
as it is in your daily existence.

The goal is not to heap up energy.
the goal is not to become a giant of Qi or Praña.
the goal is not to surpass everyone
with certain powers.

The goal is to be holy and enlightened
and thus ego-free and God-focussed.

Dissociation

Do not just learn to see others,
but yourself as well
without judgement or prejudice.

Admit and recognise your patterns
without giving in to them.

Learn to contemplate and see
the movements in your thinking, feeling and being
without moving your deepest self.

As if you were the universe,
and as if you saw yourself from the standpoint of God,
look upon yourself in meditation,
conscious,
but without thinking.

What you have to learn
is that strange difference
of awareness without thought,
of seeing without naming.

There is a conscious core within you
that remains changeless
even if everything inside you twists and turns,
even if you were nothing but chaos.

You are not your patterns,
they only arise within yourself.
You can observe them
without immediately submitting.

You have to learn to dissociate yourself
from your thoughts and actions.
You have to make that split
that makes you independent
of all the things you are addicted to.

You are not a toy
caught in the hands of certain powers
because God gave you choice
— the choice to think,
the choice to act
and the choice not to act.

Forms of meditation

There are three forms of meditation.
The one in which you focus on one point.
The one in which you focus on all points.
And the one in which you focus on no point at all.

It is your conscious core that remains unchanged
and that directs your attention
on something, everything or nothing.

It is not about consciousness in words or thoughts.
It is not about consciousness in thinking.
Neither is it about just experiencing or feeling.
But it's about looking upon and contemplating
without attaching.

It is at once contracting and letting go
of body, mind, heart and soul.

Contracts them within the object of meditation,
yet leave them free.
Do not attach them to the object of meditation
yet make them connect.

The peace of meditation originates
when neither body, mind nor heart
overwhelms the others.

Neither body, mind nor heart
should overtake the conscious core.
Your consciousness should consist of the whole
and not of a single part.

Just like love does not reduce people
but tries to see them wholly
thus your attention in meditation and prayer
should be full of love.
Contemplate
on the one, many or empty
in depth and totally
— like God looks upon your soul.

As Rabindranath Tagore said:

"You can't cross the sea merely by standing and staring at the water."

Practice

Do not cease.
Every day a little bit
is better than too much in a single moment.

Do not give up.
Rome was not build in a single day.
Neither is your soul purified in a single second.

To build is to add and to heap up.
To purify is to remove and to let go
without collapsing.
Chop off a little of the unnecessary every day.

Meditate especially when you don't feel like it at all
because downheartedness
shows the need for meditation and prayer.

A spiritually healthy person
radiates in eyes and heart.
And this glow only emerges
when one slowly gets rid
of the rubbish that darkens and hinders the inner light.

If the rubbish surfaces,
do not get scared,
do not run from it,
but face it and purify the water.
The wind will then blow waves in it
and make it flow once more.

When you're tired,
go to sleep.
When you're hungry,
go and eat.
But when your soul is hungry
or your heart has fallen asleep,
go and meditate.

God again and again takes steps
towards you.
So again and again take steps
towards Him.

Commencing

As Lao Tse said:

"One who puts himself in the spotlight is not enlightened.

One who glorifies himself is not glorious.

One who fames himself is not famous.

One who is too proud is nothing but a fraud.

On your toes you cannot stand.

With stiff legs you cannot run."

Breathing

Better breath is better life.

Breathing is the one thing you cannot do without
if you want to live.
The one who stops breathing dies.
The one who breathes shallowly fades.
The one who breathes deeply settles oneself
in the eternal breath of God.

There is no breath
but THE breath.
Given like a kiss
It blew our life within.

God blows over and in your soul.
His great force
resides in the little breeze
and not in the bigger storm.

When you breathe,
do it calmly
and become one with God's breeze.

Forget what occupied you yesterday,
forget what you have done today,
forget what will come tomorrow.

Come to your naked being.
by letting go of everything
that holds you back.

If you want to go deeper,
then first only breath matters.

For once do absolutely nothing
except breathing,
otherwise you will become a lifeless phantom
that constantly runs after itself
without ever catching that self.

You are because you breathe
and not because you think
as some think.

Humbleness

Be humble.
If you were wondrous and perfect,
you wouldn't need meditation or prayer.

Descend.
Turn within,
but without idolising yourself.

You are an image of God
but you are not God.

Admit for once that you do not always
do the right thing,
think the right thing
or say the right thing.

Admit for once that you sometimes
make mistakes,
think mistakes
and say the wrong things.

Admit for once that you often deviate
from the Divine image you could be.

God Himself on the other hand is not an image.
He does not deviate from Himself.
Mirror yourself in Him.

Contemplate your wrong actions
in the appearance of God's love,
Consider your wrong thoughts
in front of God's truth,
analyse your words
from within God's unity.

You are not always coherent.
You are not always consistent.
You want to give and receive love
but you often keep it to yourself
and often don't dare to accept it.
So don't blame God for your suffering.

In meditation and prayer
God is the point of concentration and reference.
In meditation and prayer
God is the focus and the counterweight.

His deepest peace,
which you can perceive within,
is the measuring stick
and what does not correspond to it
must be banished.

Posture

Make sure your posture is correct and stable.
Be like a rock.
Sit straight and stately.
Be like a tree.
Sit serene and relaxed.
Be like a lake.

When you notice that you weaken and slump
then correct your posture.
When you notice that your thoughts wander
then call them back.

Straighten your body.
Focus on your breathing.
Concentrate your mind.

Both your body and your mind can wander,
can slowly lose their form.
Reform your form if so.
Meditation is not relaxation.
Meditation is contemplation and concentration.

Only aimed and focussed,
both in body and mind,
shall you taste the fruit.

When you concentrate in this manner
you will soon feel a spring breeze blowing
within and around yourself.

The energy will come to straighten your back.
God's spirit will come to bring peace to your thoughts.

Pain in back and limbs can sometimes disturb.
Neither put too much strain,
nor be tempted to stop too soon.
Sit at ease,
do not wrench yourself in awkward postures
or needlessly wear out your body,
but bite through when at first it feels a uneasy.

Nothing is accomplished without effort.
And that is even more so
when it comes to inner progress.

Consciousness

Be conscious of the fact you meditate.
Be conscious of your breath.
Be conscious of your posture.
Be conscious of your consciousness.

Turn your gaze inside.

Feel your breath flow.
Feel your energy spread.
Feel your belly swell and shrink
with breath and energy.

Feel your back straighten itself.
Feel your body relax.
Feel your mind concentrate.
Feel your soul connect.

Be conscious of your meditation
and of its origin.

Be conscious
that you also have to leave behind
this consciousness.

Be open,
be humble,
be prepared to receive and give.

Be conscious of the whole
of the experience in which you are immersed.

Go swim in the ocean
that stretches itself in front of you
clear and inviting.

One point meditation

As Lord Krishna said:
"When you cannot concentrate
you have no inner peace.
And how can you be happy
without inner peace?"

A focal point outside

Focus on a single point.
The flame of a candle.
The grass that gently waves in the wind.
The sparkling sun on the water.

Like a lens you narrow the mind,
until only one point is within your scope.

What surrounds it drifts apart.
It's surrounded by emptiness,
and everything sinks into this void.

Go deeper into the focal point.
Behold the glow in the flame,
the green in the grass
or the calmness in the movement of the waves.

Be open to that on which you concentrate.
It will persistently pull you further inside.

If your thoughts wander,
then focus your mind on that single point
again and again.
Without being angry or disappointed
you can very simply bring the concentration
back to the single point you chose.

It can be a candle, the grass, sparkling waves,
but also a string of beads, an image or your breath.
It can be anything anywhere,
because God is in the heart of everything He created.

When you stick to one-ness
and let everything else disappear,
you become filled with the peace
of simplicity.

Likewise, when you stick to God,
He will come to you
and offer you His peace, full of love,
for He is the calmness
in the waves of existence.

A focal point inside

Concentrate your attention on a specific part
of your physical or energetic body.
A painful part, to heal
or a blocked part, to open.

You can focus on a chakra.
You can focus on an uneasy feeling.
You can focus on a spot your teacher advises.

It's never simply a matter of energy.
What you contract and concentrate
is not only Qi or Praña
but the whole of strength, hearth, mind and soul.
And these attain their biggest unity
in love.

So send love to the point you choose.
Send love and let it breathe.

Feel what is missing, tensioned or blocked.
And try to replenish, soften or disentangle it.

What is missed by everyone,
what softens everyone,
what disentangles everyone,
is Love.

So contract your whole being
in that one specific point
during your meditation.

Just like God contracts Himself
in every part of creation
to give it existence,
you must contract yourself with your whole being
in every inner part on which you meditate
to let it radiate.

The third eye

The point between your eyebrows
is known from old
as the third eye.

When it opens
you'll receive deeper insight
in the workings of the universe
and God.

No matter what the mind concentrates upon,
it should do so
through the third eye.

The third eye is your concentrated eye
and your concentrating eye.
Your other eyes
tempt you with the riches of the world.
But your third eye can see the beauty of Heaven.

Your eyes are dual,
and make you see good and evil.
Your third eye is single,
and makes you behold the whole
without being thrust back and forth
between black and white.

Your third eye is the energetic organ
that makes you capable
of contemplating consciously
without being dragged away in thoughts.

Whatever you concentrate upon,
do it consciously and from your third eye.
With the eyes closed you see and feel
that on which you focus
between your eyebrows.
With the eyes open you feel
how your third eye as well
beholds the picture
that shows itself in front of you.

Nature, humans and all living beings,
look upon them all with the eye
of honest and unrestrained simplicity.

A mantra

Everything moves,
everything vibrates,
everything dances.

God sings
creation into existence.

The one who finds the vibration,
the one who feels the rhythm
can let his soul whirl like a dervish
around its own axis.

God is the axis of your soul.

Some sounds vibrate deeper and more intense,
both spoken and recited within.

A sound, a word or a sentence,
in pure devotion and concentration
constantly repeated,
arouses a force
that drills through the thickest ego walls.

Repeating a mantra in waves
focuses the mind ever more intensely on the content.

So choose a mantra
of which you sense the depth.
The sentence of a prayer
or the sounds of a word
that fulfil you.

With every exhale
you blow the sound,
the vibration
and the purifying thought
into the world.
Just like God
never ceases
to penetrate creation
with His song.

As Jesus said:
"Those who do not become like a child,
cannot enter the kingdom of heaven."

Your faults

Discerning and admitting your faults
purifies heart, mind and soul.

You know very well that you make mistakes,
for once admit it straightforwardly.

Look upon your faults
and behold them.
Do not be angry.
Just leave them for what they are.
Just admit them
and be aware
that they have their origin within yourself
and that their effects return to you.

A wrong word, a wrong thought, a wrong deed
of the day itself,
or a wrong attitude, a wrong trait, a wrong emotion
that you carry with you for a longer time
— in essence they are no more than a knot
that needs to be untied.

Feel and see where they reside.
Let them soak off your soul.
Look upon yourself
as if you were no longer connected to these faults.
Give them to God
out of sincere repentance.

A force will fill you
as soon as you turn your back on your faults
and are willing to apologise.

Know that you are not your faults
and leave them behind,
every time again.
Even if you fall repeatedly,
stand up again and again
and refocus on becoming a being without inner friction
— a being that meditates and breathes
and knows that God exists.

Your existence is meant to be pure,
so leave your faults of thinking, doing and not-doing.

Your goodness

Discerning and admitting your good sides
can be life-giving.

You know very well that you are a child of God,
for once be very sure about it.

Look upon your radiating qualities
and behold them.
But do not lose yourself in excessive vanity.
Leave them for what they are.
Just admit them
and be aware
of how they have their origin within yourself
and how their effects return to you.

A right word, a nice thought, a pleasant deed
of the day itself,
or a right attitude, a nice trait, a pleasant emotion
that you carry with you for a longer time
— do not hinder them.
Let them blossom like a flower opening its petals
in the light of the morning sun.

Feel and see where they reside.
Let them flow further into your soul.
Look upon yourself
as if your radiating qualities became bigger.
Give them to God
out of sincere striving.

A force will fill you
as soon as you give yourself over to goodness
and are prepared to persist in it.

Know that you do not consist
solely of your good qualities
but that they spring from a pure heart.

You might forget it repeatedly,
but purify your heart again and again
and always let yourself be filled
by that which glows from within.

Breathe, meditate
and know that you exist in God
like God exists in you.

A problem

When you wrestle with a certain problem,
when you're stuck in a certain tension,
do not flee from it.

Fear or disheartenment
won't bring you solutions.

Contemplate the problem.
Take it in,
but do not let it take you over.

When it isn't clear
what exactly hinders your heart or soul,
then first come to the calmness of the breath,
and the calmness of the posture of your meditation.

Feel deeply and intensely where in your body
it manifests itself.
Feel deeply and intensely where in your mind
it manifests itself.
Feel deeply and intensely where in your heart
it manifests itself.

What is it connected to?
Who is it connected with?
Which history and which feelings are tied to it?

Untie the knot
without judging
or condemning.

See from within your conscious core,
and contemplate on every aspect
piece by piece.
Figure out how they fit the puzzle.

See from within your conscious core,
and drill to the bottom of your mind
until you find the residence of the strongest tension.

Get rid of the tension
through concentration on a self without attachment.
Open yourself to God
and leave your old and suffocating patterns.

Forgiving

Healing a disturbed relationship
starts with removing
your own part in the disturbance
— and always a certain part is yours.

Focus your attention
also on those
to whom you never send a good thought.
Focus your love
also on those
who you don't consider to deserve that love.

Get rid of your vengeance, jealousy or fear
— and in most cases, all three of them.

Let the unloved
exist in all freedom
by contemplating on him or her without prejudice.

Let go of the unloved
by not reducing him or her
to that trait which you consider to be wrong.

Let go of your contempt
and liberate both the unloved and yourself.

Like God constantly gives everyone the choice
to exist or not
you must allow everyone to be the way they are.

Those who do not reside within the limits of existence,
those who do not walk the paths of God,
will ruin themselves.
That is not something you have to take care of.

But all those who got lost in life
have a need for renewed love.
You can take care of that.

Calm your mind
by forgiving
and forgive
by calming your mind.

As Vinoba Bhave said:

"Knowledge alone is not enough. It can burn down gross impurities in the mind, but is powerless to wash away subtler impurities. The subtle impurities can be washed away only by the waters of loving devotion."

A loved one

Focus on a loved one.
Send your beloved all your love.

Your father, mother, brother, sister, friend or partner
in body or soul,
with each of them you can connect.

Connect yourself
and send what is needed, asked or wanted.

Give your love
as if it were the love that God gives you.

Be sure of the fact
that your love reaches its goal.
Be sure that the other will feel it.
Be sure that what you radiate is perceivable.

Death nor life
are a limit.
The only limit is God,
and He is infinite and eternal.

Time nor distance
matter whatsoever.
Your concentration and dedication
will determine the force.
Your connection
goes as far and as deep
as you yourself allow.

The image of a saint

Look upon an image
of a great saint, an enlightened being or a prophet,
of a son or daughter of God,
of a soul that shines eternally and clarifies the world
with its death-transcending existence.

Contemplate the image
and take it in.

Let it grow,
and let it overtake your complete consciousness,
as a whole
or through every aspect of the image.

Contemplate on the one that hides behind the image
and how he or she connects with you.

Let his or her light
penetrate your whole existence.
Hear his or her whispering words
and try to accord your being
with the life and being of the surpassing one.

Contemplate how the one that hides behind the image
was embedded and rooted in God.
and how it makes him or her
stretch throughout the world.

Let his or her presence
lead your existence further into the Divine
by concentrating on his or her transcendence
or by perceiving the inviting Divinity
that shines in all of those
who were reunited with their Creator.

Even without an image
one only has to close one's eyes
and inwardly recall their image
to make them present.
Because those who are absorbed in God
are always and everywhere just as near as God Himself.

Unity meditation

As Kabir said:

"Many know that the parts are contained in the whole but only few know that the whole is also contained in every part."

Perceiving unity

Go and sit in nature.
Open your eyes
and let everything in front of you
exist the way it is.

Do not give names to what you see,
do not create distinctions
between what you hear, smell or feel.

Let your point of concentration be the whole
of everything that surrounds you.

You don't have to put anything or anyone
in compartments
because the border
between yourself and the other
is a border you drew yourself.

Lift all borders
by letting the whole flow and exist
as one great creation
that flows from the Creator
and returns to the Creator.

Practice in seeing that
which constitutes the unity
in and between everything.

Practice in looking at everything
without the distinction
others once gave to it.

Practice in contemplating on the world
as it is
and not as you would like it to be.

Focus on nothing
by taking in everything all at once
— and then feel
how you are taken up in the whole.

Let all reference to objects go,
because everything ultimately refers
to the One subject
that, like a waterfall,
drenches the world
with love.

From your core to the whole

You are here and now.
You're nowhere else and at no other moment.

Nevertheless you have also always been,
you always will be,
and you reach further then you dare to guess
because you're connected to God.

Be conscious of the moment
and the place you take in it.
Be conscious that your core
meditates immovably
yet finds itself always surrounded by change.

Focus on what surrounds you.
Enlarge your circle of space.
Feel around you
as if your body is also there
where it's not.

Open yourself
and try to envelop what surrounds you.
Let all existence flow through you.

Experience the garden in which you sit,
the room in which you meditate,
or the temple in which you pray.

Rise out.
Stretch your soul beyond your surroundings.

As if you were reaching for God with all your being,
expand yourself
and take in everything.

Without judgement,
without good or evil,
you become the wind that blows over the grass
or the sun that sparkles in the water.

Feel and experience what surrounds you.
Feel and experience how you are rooted in it.
It is a fertile ground full of energy
that gives you the opportunity to grow to God.

From the whole to your core

Everything is connected.
And you have a place in everything.

Look upon yourself from the Whole.
Look upon yourself as if you had the eyes of God.
Look upon yourself and contemplate your being.
Consider the path that lies in front of you.

Look upon your connectedness
with the history and the world.
You have a place in it,
you have a reason and a meaning.
Consider these from the Whole.

Feel deeply,
feel deeply within your heart,
feel deeply with your entire being
feel deeply how you can fit in the Whole.

Everything has the same fundament
and yet
nothing or nobody
can replace you
or take over your task.

Don't breathe only air,
Don't breathe only energy
but breathe God and His omnipresence.

Don't breathe only air,
don't breathe only energy
but breathe love and willpower.

You are creation that has taken form.
Contemplate on creation and see
how you are created over and over,
and how your soul helps to create creation.

Like God always transcends
and at the same time incarnates,
thus you always have to
let the Whole flow through you
so you can pave your way through the world
like a river.

Flowing thoughts

Let thoughts come and go.
Find the holes between the thoughts
and dive into them.

Do not be angry with yourself
when your mind is full of thoughts.
You only have to let them disappear
the way they surfaced
— like waves in the sea of your consciousness.

When you do not cling to thoughts
they receive their place and time.
When your mind does not cramp on certain ideas
and your heart does not cramp on certain feelings
your soul finds peace.

Do not give more weight
to certain thoughts or feelings.
Only be the spectator of the waves of your mind.

All thoughts and feelings are connected
and where they connect
a small emptiness arises,
a little gateway to thoughtlessness.

Thoughtlessness
is the whole of all thoughts
in which they come and go.

Thoughtlessness
is your conscious core
in which all thinking and feeling originate
and to which they return.

Control your thoughts and feelings
from your conscious core.
Otherwise you'll be controlled by them
and become their slave.

Let all your thoughts and feelings
be carried by God's love.
Let them find their true aim
and attain their peace
in the glowing whole of your existence.

As the Qur'an states:

"Wherever you turn is the face of God."

The questions of life

In God all answers are present.
The one who meditates deeply on certain questions
will eventually find an answer.

Wisdom is just as much around you
as the air you breathe.
Truth can be found where you're open to it.

It isn't so
that everybody has his truth,
but everybody has his view on truth.
You are embedded in truth,
it is only difficult to see the whole.

All questions that life brings up
can be answered by placing them
within the whole
and by facing it's foundation of unity.

Concentrate on the question,
and its relation to the whole.
Contemplate on the question from the whole
as if you considered it with God's eyes.

Dig deeper into the question
and be open to a whispering answer.

Dig deeper into the question
by not answering immediately.

Dig deeper into the question
and experience how the answer slowly
anchors itself into what you knew.

Dialogue with God
and the ones that walked His paths until the very end.
They always answer
those who turn to them in humbleness.

Meditate on what was said by
prophets and sages
until you understand what they meant.
Find the unity in the paradoxes
which their words seemingly procured.
Find the wisdom in the foolishness
which a life in and for God seemingly brings.

In love, no loneliness

The one who feels abandoned,
the one who feels lonely,
the one who feels lost
must look for himself in God,
must learn how God is always around
and must experience how love never leaves
unless he refuses to give love
out of his own free choice.

In God there is no loneliness
since God is the flow
from love to love
because of love.

In the greater love
that always surrounds you
you have your share
and right to existence.

If a certain love is taken from you
then refocus on the infinity of God's love
and rediscover the peace of pure being.

From the greater whole of love
that always surrounds you
your life and existence gets meaning,
not from the limited love
that was given to you temporarily.

Contemplate the way in which you must,
in this life,
give form to love in your own way.

Contemplate the way in which you have,
in this life,
been given a task within the greater love.

Contemplate the way in which you can,
in this life,
give back to Creation.

Thus you shall never lack love
because your existence will be carried
by God Himself.

Get rid of all the tensions
that spring from the twisted love
with which you desperately wish
to attach others to yourself.

Give yourself freedom
by freeing others.

Pain in the heart is best healed
by letting the soul flow
to God.

Emptiness meditation

As Jalal ad-Din Rumi said:
"Your task is not to seek for love, but merely to seek and find all the barriers within yourself that you have built against it."

The one who cannot empty himself
can never be filled.

Cut off the excessive,
throw out the unnecessary.

Be centred around your centre.
Be like a rock.
Be immovable.
And breathe.

Leave a space between every cycle of breath.
After every exhale, wait just a little,
and stop your thoughts.

Empty your head
by mercilessly throwing out all thoughts.
Empty your heart
by not giving any importance to your emotions.
Empty your soul
by considering all experiences as nothing more
than different modes of being.

To only breathe
is at once the most simple
and the most difficult.
Do not give up.

Constantly you are attacked
by your own thoughts, emotions and ego.
Do not give up.

Continue.
Neither pain nor confusion
should make you quit with drilling
until you experience emptiness,
see emptiness,
taste emptiness.

Do not suppress.
Do not push away.
But empty your cup
and let go.

Bring everything to rest
by detaching yourself of everything
and by being in non-doing.

Prayer

As Jesus said:

"Ask and it will be given to you, seek and you will find, knock and the door will be opened. What kind of father would give his child a snake if it asked for a fish? Or a scorpion if it asked for an egg? If you then, treat your children like this, why would God not give the Holy Spirit to those who ask for it?"

To ask

Examine your soul,
find out what you need
and be humble enough
to ask for it.

Examine your soul,
find out what you need
but let go of that
which springs from ego-desire.

Examine your soul,
find out what you need
and acknowledge
that God can give it.

Aim your questions like an arrow.
Be clear and know what you ask for.

The one who asks doubting and insecure,
will get a doubtful and uncertain answer.

Ask from your heart and soul.
Ask for purification and healing.
Ask for clarity on your path
and for strength in walking it.

But do not ask from your ego.
Do not ask to hurt others.
Do not ask to mislead others.
Do not ask to weaken others.
Do not ask to possess what is not yours.
Such questions lead away from God
and your own core.

For God does not fulfil your longing,
He fulfils your need.

So ask in purity for purity
and thank God
out of faith
that you immediately received
what you asked for.

To praise

The task of the angels is
to eternally sing praise of God
and drink His love.

The one who wants to bathe in the light of God
must only realise
that God already surrounds him.

The one who wants to bathe in the light of God
must only thank God
and sing His praise like angels.

The one who wants to bathe in the light of God
must only open up
and drink His love.

A song of praise will spontaneously emerge
from your inner being
when you start feeling enveloped by God's light.

Your mantra will become pure love
that you want to send to God
like a kiss.

Thanking
opens your inner lungs
and lets you breathe deeply again.

Thanking
interrupts al your judging
and brings fresh air.

Thanking
learns to love beauty
because of beauty itself.

To live in love because of God
is to thank Him truly.

To thank God for what one has
is to break the ego that wants ever more
with a hammer of softness.

To pray for others

Pray for your soul.
Pray for your loved ones.
Pray for peace.
Pray for a world which is being destroyed.
Pray for those who can't find love.
Pray for souls that lost themselves.

Pray for everything that needs love
— and in fact everything needs love.

Send your love
and ask God for support.
Try to be near and present with your soul,
embrace and hug with your spiritual arms.
Give freedom
and send strength.

To keep others in mind like God would do,
that is to pray.

When your spirit occupies itself uncontrollably
with one specific person
— through memories, deliberation or judgement —
then break your confused thinking
by praying for that person
and leaving everything else as it is.

Although everybody has the choice
to ignore them,
your prayers always reach their goal,
because God is the messenger
of every truthful prayer.

When you pray for something or someone else,
you learn to abandon egoism,
and to break egocentrism.

When you pray for something or someone else,
you learn to give like God does,
and you learn to take others in your heart,
like God shelters every soul.

To recite prayers

When you recite your prayers
you should do so with full conviction
and contemplation.

To mumble words
is of no use at all.
Inattentively recited words
have no force at all.

Every thought in prayer
should be fully dedicated to God
or your neighbour.

When you pray prayers
you should do so with full consciousness
and understanding.

You should mindfully chew on every word,
only then can you digest it in love
and use it as firewood for your soul.

To repeat prayers out of mere habit
or to recite them out of obligation
breaks down more than it builds up.
It blunts the mind
by not comprehending what you do.

Every prayer is inner
even when shouted out.

Read and spoken from the soul
prayer can direct your mind like a spear.

The wisdom and surrender of those who preceded you
are contained in their prayers.
Their words
can direct your wisdom and devotion to God.
Their prayers
can open your soul.

Sincerely repeated prayers
allow God
to drill Himself deeper and deeper into your heart.

As Clement of Alexandria said:

"Live life in joy. Be convinced that God is always present and be aware that you are never separated from Him."

To devote yourself

Give yourself over to God
so God can give Himself to you.

He who does nothing from the ego,
but always lets God act through him,
gets everything done.

Leave your craving and wanting
and become an instrument of love.

If you're truly serious
that you love your loved ones,
then let God lead you
because then you'll be able to serve them best.

Focussed on yourself,
focussed on what you think is best,
focussed on what you desire,
you are only capable of creating your own little world.

Focussed on God,
focussed on what is best for others,
focussed on what your soul has to do,
you can join in the creation of existence.

Ask God
to take you in
and let God
reveal Himself through you.

Your ego brought you the suffering
that afflicted yourself.
Why then would you trust it more than God?

The egos of others brought the misery
that afflicted the world.
Why then would you trust them more than God?

In trust and devotion
God unties the knot of your soul
that is called the ego.

Through trust and surrender
you burn the roughest impurities of your soul
in the Holy fire.

To unify

When nothing but love remains,
when only an ocean of peaceful existence
stretches itself in front of you,
when all disappears in one wavy motion
from love to love
because of love.

When you taste sweetness,
and everything gleams and buzzes of pure caress,
when everything vibrates and dances
and shines in one glow
of the finest dust of existence.

When giving becomes receiving
and attaining becomes spreading,
when life becomes a kiss of unity
and the lover nests in his Beloved.

When you see nothing else
than your Beloved
and when you feel nothing else
than the gaze of your Beloved
on your existence.

When every drop and every tree
take the face of your Beloved,
when every sigh of wind
and the moon as well
love you as much as you love them.

When you know
that you are created
out of everything that surrounds you,
that you exist
out of all the beauty pulled together.

When you can sincerely say
I lose myself in You
without being lost.

Then God prays in you
and you in God.

To be at peace

Whatever you do,
if you fill it with God,
then you are praying.

Whatever you do,
if you dedicate it to God,
then you are praying.

Whatever you do,
if you let God's love go in front of you,
then you are praying.

Whatever you feel,
if you sense its relation to God,
then you are praying.

Whatever you think,
if you contemplate within God,
then you are praying.

Whatever you want,
if you leave it to God,
then you are praying.

Whatever you expect,
if you put your trust in God,
then you are praying.

The one who expects nothing
or isn't worried about results,
acts out of pure love.

The one who wants nothing
or isn't afraid to lose,
acts because of the other.

The one who doesn't think evil
or doesn't judge quickly,
acts out of love for existence and truth.

The one who returns to God
again and again,
to question and correct
his doing and not-doing
his thinking, feeling and striving
finds peace within the soul.

Concluding

As Abu Sa'id ibn Abi al-Khayr said:
"The true saint moves amongst people, eats and sleeps with them, buys and sells on the market, gets married and takes part in the social life, and never forgets God for a single moment."

End your meditation or prayer
by descending in your body.

Let your replenished soul
and your clarified mind
rain into every cell.

Let the peace in your heart
softly flow through your veins.

Become conscious again of your body
and your surrounding
— draw your consciousness back into the world.

Open your posture
and look upon the world with a purified vision.

While you stretch yourself
you also stretch out
the experience of your meditation
within your body.

When an inner wrestling
did not find its finality,
simply resolve to continue later
for you will not be enlightened in one meditation
and you will not be holy because of one good deed.

Let your prayer vibrate
in your body, heart, mind and soul.

Let your meditation and prayer
flow into every action
big or small.

Let God work through you
in all your thoughts
big or small.

Let your whole life slowly become
meditation and prayer
in which every event and every contact
becomes a kiss
from God to you
and from you to God.

As St. Francis de Sales said:

"Meditate or pray at least half an hour a day.
Unless you're occupied with too many things.
Then meditate or pray at least an hour."

About Yunus Publishing

Yunus Publishing produces books and webprojects on religion, mysticism and politics.

To be informed of future releases
If you would like to be informed of new publications, please subscribe to the newsletter on *www.yunuspublishing.org*. You will only be contacted when a new book or web project is launched, your address will never be shared and you can unsubscribe at any time.

A kind request
Word-of-mouth is of course crucial for any type of publication. So, if you enjoyed this book, please consider leaving a review at the retailer where you obtained it. Even if it's only a line or two, it can be a huge help for a small publishing house like ours.

Contact
For any comment, question or request you're always welcome to send an e-mail to *mail@yunuspublishing.org*.

www.yunuspublishing.org
www.jonasatlas.net

www.ingramcontent.com/pod-product-compliance
Lightning Source LLC
Chambersburg PA
CBHW032136040426
42449CB00005B/267